KEEPSAKE CHRISTMAS STORIES

KEEPSAKE
CHRISTMAS
STORIES

HOLIDAY FAVORITES AS PERFORMED WITH
The Tabernacle Choir

SHADOW
MOUNTAIN

THE
TABERNACLE
CHOIR AT TEMPLE SQUARE

The Tabernacle Choir at Temple Square provides artistic expressions of faith from The Church of Jesus Christ of Latter-day Saints.

Text and photographs © 2021 by Intellectual Reserve, Inc. All rights reserved.
See page 120 for acknowledgments, author/adapter credits, and other copyright information.

Photographs on pages 40, 48, 51, 66–67, 84, and 110 © Deseret News Publishing Company.

Visit us at ShadowMountain.com

Library of Congress Cataloging-in-Publication Data
CIP on file.

ISBN 978-1-62972-939-8

Printed in the United States of America
Lake Book Manufacturing, Inc., Melrose Park, IL

10   9   8   7   6   5   4   3   2   1

CONTENTS

STORIES OF WONDER

There's something *wonderful* about a good story at Christmas. Literally. When the Yule log burns low and the twinkling lights on the tree sparkle with joy, the words "Once upon a time" truly evoke a sense of wonder. Which is why, for twenty years, the annual Christmas concert of The Tabernacle Choir has featured a holiday story.

Some of the stories have been traditional favorites, but most have been original, adapted from classic literature, or drawn from the pages of history. Wherever they come from, each of the stories is presented with a specially composed score performed by the Orchestra at Temple Square, often incorporating a beloved carol or a new Christmas song sung by the Choir. It's this unique union of story, instrumental music, and song that makes each presentation memorable.

For those who plan the concerts, it's hard to be certain which comes first, the theme of the concert or the choice of the story. Both have been influenced by the Choir's guest artists—award-winning singers, actors, authors, and newscasters who share the stage with the Choir and Orchestra each year. For example, who better to tell the story of World War I's Christmas truce than Walter Cronkite? And could anyone be more poised to unfold the English carol "Good King Wenceslas" than British actress Jane Seymour? Pearl S. Buck's story of a Depression-era farm boy was a perfect fit for Richard Thomas, not only because of his portrayal of John-Boy in *The Waltons* television series, but because he spent his childhood summers on his grandparents' eastern Kentucky farm. And so it goes—year after year, artist and story come together, reflecting and inspiring the musical program that has made the concert the most watched holiday special on PBS for over a decade.

Through the years, some of these stories have been available in picture books and smaller volumes. Others have never been published. Because readers continue to ask for them, The Tabernacle Choir and its publishing partner, Shadow Mountain, are pleased to offer this keepsake treasury along with a special invitation.

The full wonder of these stories is best experienced beyond the printed page. As you open the covers of this book, we invite you to also open a digital device and visit the address listed below. There you will find several videos of the stories as they were presented in concert—complete with enchanting sets and costumes, historical and animated images projected on giant screens, parachutes falling from the sky, and characters flying high above the audience.

We hope that the compelling performances of renowned narrators and soaring cinematic soundtracks, along with over 500 Choir and Orchestra members singing and playing from their souls, warms your heart and lightens your spirit.

So, let the fire burn low and the tree sparkle with joy. There is something *wonderful* about these stories at Christmas. Literally.

Selected Christmas Stories from The Tabernacle Choir
TabChoir.org/KeepsakeChristmas

*In this edition, lyrics are set in italics and were sung by
The Tabernacle Choir when the story was presented in concert.
Some of the stories have been adapted for print and do not
reflect an exact transcript of the original performance.*

SILENT NIGHT, HOLY NIGHT

The Story of the World War I Christmas Truce

NARRATED BY WALTER CRONKITE

The 1900s, the final century of the recent millennium, brought unprecedented possibilities and promise.

The children of these hundred years would see more improvement in the human condition than ever before in the world's history.

Advances in medicine, science, and industry would all but eradicate disease, extend human life, open a dialogue among the peoples of the earth, and lift them into the vast reaches of space.

But these hardly seemed like possibilities as the Christmas of 1914 drew near.

The nations of Europe were at war. Anxious to expand and defend their borders, they summoned their best and brightest to the battlefront. Young men answered by the millions.

A nineteen-year-old German boy left his job in London to enlist in the German army. English boys working and studying in Hamburg and Paris returned to London, put on their uniforms, and went back to fire upon former friends.

Secretary of War, Lord Kitchener, expanded the British army overnight by allowing schoolmates to enlist together.

The tragedy of these battalions was no more evident than at Somme, France. Hundreds of villages on both sides lost almost all their young men in a single battle. The little paybook that every British soldier carried included a last will and testament.

Thousands of these booklets were collected from the bodies of young boys, many reading simply, "I leave everything to my mother."

With hardly a backward glance, the promise of youth was poured into the blind and futile aggression known as the Great War, World War I.

The new century brought a new kind of warfare. Field commanders quickly realized that digging in was the only way to survive the sweep of machine-gun fire.

The German army had marched across Belgium before being stopped at Flanders Field. Some sixty yards away, British, French, and Belgian troops languished in trenches infested with rats and lice; pelted with freezing rain and shrapnel. As temperatures dropped, disease took hold. Snipers picked off any who raised their heads above the earthen wall. The war was but four months old, each side losing thousands a day, both to bullets and that silent, common enemy: influenza.

Between the opposing trenches was an area about the width of a football field: No Man's Land. Littered with barbed wire and frozen corpses, it was a sobering reminder of what the future might bring. Soldiers who survived later recalled their dead brothers being gathered up and stacked like cords of wood. By war's end, over ten million would be lost.

Not surprisingly, given the circumstances, most of the soldiers were religious; and many were Christian. On Sundays, communion was passed in trenches on both sides, often to the sound of church bells ringing in nearby villages. The occasional hymn was sung, and youthful voices were heard across enemy lines.

By December, the war slowed and hopes for a quick resolution faded away. As the soldiers contemplated their desperate situation, nights grew long and hearts yearned for peace.

December twenty-third. A group of German soldiers quietly moved to the ruins of a bombed-out monastery. There, they held their Christmas service.

Later on that night, a few Christmas trees, *Tannenbaums* as they were called, began to appear along the German fortifications, their tiny candles flickering in the night.

Across the way, British soldiers took an interest in those lights as they sang together the carols of their youth. Word spread, and heads peeked cautiously over sandbags at the now thousands of Tannenbaums glowing like Christmas stars.

Two British officers ventured over to the German line and, against orders, arranged a Christmas truce. But the negotiation was a mere formality by then. Up and down the trenches men from both sides already had begun crossing the line to join the celebration.

Lieutenant Sir Edward Hulse "assaulted" the enemy with music. In a letter to his mother he wrote, "We are going to give the enemy every conceivable song . . . from carols to Tipperary."

The Germans responded with a Christmas concert of their own. It was not long before the cold air rang with everything from "Good King Wenceslas" to "Auld Lang Syne."

For the next two days, those tidings continued to spring from the hearts of common men who shared the common bond of Christmas.

Further down the line, a German violinist stood atop his parapet, framed against the skeletons of bare trees and shattered fortifications. Delicately perched in this desolate landscape, his cold fingers conveyed the poignant beauty of Handel's *Largo*.

Whatever the spirit of Christmas had been before that hour, it was now, above all, the spirit of hope, of peace.

A British war correspondent reported that later the soldiers heard a clear voice singing the French carol, "O Holy Night." The singer: Victor Granier of the Paris Opera. The night watch must have lifted their eyes toward the heavens as they heard his plaintive call.

Christmas Day dawned over the muddy fields, and both sides cautiously picked their way through the barbed wire. Side by side they buried their dead.

A German officer known only as Thomas gave Lieutenant Hulse a Christmas gift: a Victoria cross and letter which had belonged to an English captain. Lieutenant Hulse responded by giving the German officer his silk scarf.

One German retrieved a photograph of himself in uniform and asked his former enemies to post it to his sister in Liverpool.

Men who had shot at each other only days before gathered in a sacred service for their fallen brothers. Prayers were offered, and the twenty-third Psalm was read:

The Lord is my shepherd; I shall not want.

He maketh me to lie down in green pastures: he leadeth me beside the still waters.

He restoreth my soul: he leadeth me in the paths of righteousness for his name's sake.

Yea, though I walk through the valley of the shadow of death, I will fear no evil: for thou art with me; thy rod and thy staff they comfort me.

Thou preparest a table before me in the presence of mine enemies: thou anointest my head with oil; my cup runneth over.

Surely goodness and mercy shall follow me all the days of my life: and I will dwell in the house of the Lord for ever.

Nineteen-year-old Arthur Pelham-Burn, who hoped to study for the ministry after the war ended, remembered: "The Germans formed up on one side, the English on the other, the officers standing in front, every head bared. Yes, I think it is a sight one will never see again."

As the Christmas of 1914 drew to a close, soldiers who had sung together, played together, and prayed together, returned to their trenches. They must have felt reluctant to let the common ground between them become No Man's Land again. But as the darkness fell around them, a lone voice floated across the few yards of earth on which they had stood together. In the true spirit of Christmas, one voice, then another, joined in. Soon, the whole world seemed to be singing. And, for a brief moment, the sound of peace was a carol every soul knew by heart.

Silent night! Holy night!
All is calm, all is bright
Round yon virgin mother and Child.
Holy Infant, so tender and mild,
Sleep in heavenly peace;
Sleep in heavenly peace.

Silent night! Holy night!
Shepherds quake at the sight!
Glories stream from heaven afar;
Heav'nly hosts sing Alleluia!
Christ, the Savior, is born!
Christ, the Savior, is born!

Silent night! Holy Night!
Son of God, love's pure light
Radiant beams from thy holy face,
With the dawn of redeeming grace,
Jesus, Lord, at thy birth;
Jesus, Lord, at thy birth.

And that's the way it was, one silent night almost a hundred years ago; and that's the way it can be as each of us embraces the message of that silent, holy night.

AFTERWORD

There are many details in war stories; some contribute to good storytelling, while other are just interesting. Omitting some of these details was perhaps the most difficult part of assembling this true story. Each detail brought gravity to a heavy war and made the Christmas truce all that more profound. Throughout December, gifts—English puddings and German chocolate—were heaved from trench to trench. A German boot exploded in an English trench, stuffed with sausages, chocolate, and cigars. There were soccer games in No Man's Land. A British soldier captured a rabbit, and soldiers from both sides contributed tins of vegetables and meat to make a batch of Christmas stew. It hardly seemed possible at the time that the war would last so long.

But the conflict turned into a long, brutal war. The industrial revolution spawned machinery capable of killing thousands at a time. In the end, not only would ten million die but the tenuous peace led to bitterness and shame that influenced the Second World War.

Still, for a time, young Londoners who had befriended German waiters and German patrons of French operas saw the war as something temporary. They didn't really hate each other in the first few months. In was only out of duty that they fought. So when an opportunity to celebrate a common holiday arose, so did the men from their trenches.

The guns were silent for a day. And when soldiers from both sides returned to their trenches after Christmas and the command to resume was issued, they would fire only at the clouds. The war was stalled until replacements were rotated in.

A CHRISTMAS BELL FOR ANYA

An Original Russian Christmas Tale

NARRATED BY CLAIRE BLOOM

If it is true that you appreciate most what you don't often have, then the people of Listbolski, Russia, loved the warmth of the spring more than any other people on earth.

The Siberian winters were long, cold, bitter, and mercilessly dark. Week after week, the snow would gather, until the Sayan Mountains around the village were an unending blanket of smooth, white snow. The skies were almost always gray and lifeless, though there were occasional days when the north wind would blow, clearing the air to an eye-piercing blue.

The people of Listbolski lived simple lives. They didn't have a lot—a little wood for their fires, a little oil for their lamps. They didn't expect very much, yet they always had hope. And they had their families. And that seemed to be enough.

During the winter of 1917, the entire state of Russia had fallen into dark and tumultuous times, as the reign of the Czars came to a terrible, violent end. What was to replace it, the people of Listbolski didn't know, but rumors of marauding soldiers and war had reached the village, leaving the villagers with dark concerns to fill the long nights.

Anya was eight years old when she became aware of the violent upheaval around her. Though she was young, she was particularly sensitive for her age, and she knew, sometimes even more than the others, that a great danger was near.

Through the long winter, she and her father would often sit next to their fire, talking

and listening to the cold wind blow outside. On these evenings, her father would some-times gaze at her and think, *So much like her mother. The same bright smile. The same dark eyes.*

He loved Anya more than anything he had left in this world.

Though Listbolski was but a small village, there was one thing it was famous for. You see, the village artisans created the finest Christmas bells in the world, the red brass producing the clearest sound one could hear. Because of this, Listbolski had a Christmas tradition that went back many generations. Each year, the newest baby boy from the village was selected to represent the Christ child. On Christmas morning, he would be wrapped in a blanket and laid in a manger in the town square. Twelve village girls, dressed as angels, were selected to stand around the child, each of them sounding her bell to ring in Christmas morn.

The year she turned eight, Anya was selected to be one of the angels standing beside the Christ child. Out of all the children in the village, she was one of the few! As Christmas approached, she lay awake, the blankets pulled completely over the top of her head, dreaming of the morning when she would ring her own bell.

For weeks her father labored feverishly, knowing the final product had to be his very best work. Finally, just three days before Christmas, he brought Anya's bell home.

With his excited daughter on his knee, he laid his tools on the table and, working together, they etched these words into the smooth metal on the inside of the bell: "For My Angel to Ring on Christmas Morn."

Anya watched, her eyes blazing, as her father etched the words. Then she picked up the bell and held it as if it were made of pure gold.

Turning to her father, she put her slender arms around his neck. "I really want to ring my bell Christmas morning," she said.

He nodded at her happily. "I know that you do."

"I love you, Father," she whispered as she clutched her bell.

That night they came. Half an army, half a mob, they tore through the village with a dark and hateful fury.

They set fires. They killed and they randomly destroyed. Then they rode away on their horses, their flaming torches illuminating the night.

Morning found Anya's father weeping over his child. He had wrapped her in a blanket and held her until her tiny body was cold. As the glow of the fire faded, he looked up and cried, "God, why my daughter? Why my child?!"

For two days he sat alone on his wooden chair. He didn't eat. He didn't sleep. He hardly had the will to breathe.

Afraid of the anger and the pain that was consuming him, his soul cried out in anguish and loneliness. Enveloped by such darkness and without any strength, he did the only thing he could. Moving beneath his pain toward the small ember still burning within him, he whispered, "Thank you, God, for letting me be Anya's father for eight years. Thank you for the afternoon she helped me etch the words on her bell." For a moment, his simple acceptance seemed to soften his grief. The night passed, and the day finally came, finding him still alone.

He listened to the village outside his home coming to life; the sound of people, some of them singing, then children's voices. Hard as their lot had become, the villagers knew they had to go on with their lives.

He forced himself to his feet and turned toward his cottage door. Numb and silent, he slowly walked to the village square. Gathering with the others, he knelt at the manger of the Christ child, then lifted his eyes to the angels, each of them holding a bell. And as the young girls began their ringing, he listened to the pealing of the bells and knew that the message of Christmas was real.

The sound of the bells slowly faded, and the silence of the mountains returned. The villagers tarried, reluctant to break the spirit of that Christmas morning; but the cold eventually drove them back to their homes, the sounds of their footsteps muffled by the newly fallen snow, leaving Anya's father alone at the manger.

At last, he turned and started walking away from the square when, lifting his eyes to the morning light, he suddenly stopped.

He didn't see her, but he knew; somehow he knew that Anya was near.

Then he felt her whisper the message she wanted him to hear. "He was born, Father, so that I might live. I'm still living, Father, and I'll be waiting for you."

He fell to his knees in the snow, overcome with relief and gratitude. A sudden warmth seemed to fill him as her words touched his heart. "Ring the bell for me, Father. Ring it every Christmas morn. He was born and He lives now. So think of Him. Think of me. And ring our bell every Christmas morn."

LONGFELLOW'S CHRISTMAS

The Inspiring Origins of "I Heard the Bells on Christmas Day"

NARRATED BY EDWARD HERRMANN

In the winter of 1860, Cambridge, Massachusetts, captures the essence of an American Christmas. Under starry skies and between snow-laden pines, proud New England houses push their way through a thick white blanket. Their yellow-orange windows, like Christmas candles, are reflected in the ice-bound Charles River.

In the silence of falling snow, sleigh bells and laughter crescendo as the Longfellow family, bundled in winter wool, is whisked along behind glossy horses. And above them, a thousand bare branches release a shower of sparkling snow. Five children giggle with delight. And ringing down cobbled lanes, across fields and through the wooded hills and valleys, are the bells—single steeple bells and bundles of carillon bells—playing those old familiar carols that make Christmas . . . *Christmas*. To men and women of good will everywhere, this is the music of hope and peace.

The following year, 1861, America will need that music to counter the drum and bugle of civil war. Rising from the strife are the plaintive songs of divided families— songs for lively boys who steal off to war, and broken young men carried back to their homes and, too often, on to early graves.

Still, for the Longfellow family of Cambridge, summer comes as it always has. For the five children, outings to the seashore, long walks under leafy canopies, and happy hours in the family home seem to promise that this summer will not, cannot, end.

Then on Tuesday, July ninth, a fire in the Longfellow home claims the life of the children's mother, Fanny. Trying to rescue her, her husband, Henry, is severely burned on his hands and face. Three days later, Fanny, his beloved wife, is buried on the eighteenth anniversary of their wedding day, while he is confined to his bed, fighting to live—fighting to *want* to live. For Henry Wadsworth Longfellow, as one war rages without, another rages within.

For the next two years, Christmases come and go. Henry writes, "How inexpressibly sad are all the holidays. 'A merry Christmas' say the children, but that is no more for me. Perhaps someday God will give me peace."

And then Henry learns that his eldest son, Charles, who ran away to join the army, has been critically wounded in battle. Henry rushes to Washington to bring his son home, and after days of searching, he finds him—barely alive.

With the outbreak of war, Fanny's terrible death, and now, two years later, his son desperately clinging to life, we should not be surprised that on Christmas Day, 1863, Henry reaches for his pen and writes:

> *It was as if an earthquake rent*
> *The hearthstones of a continent.*
> *And in despair I bowed my head:*
> *"There is no peace on earth," I said,*
> *"For hate is strong and mocks the song*
> *Of peace on earth, good will to men."*

Reading his words today, we ask: When conflict rages and pain, grief, and loneliness overwhelm us, where is the music of hope and peace?

For Henry, the answer to that question has everything to do with Christmas. After Fanny's death, he had written: "So strong is the sense of her presence upon me, that I should hardly be surprised to look up now and see her in the room. Death is a beginning, not an end."

On that Christmas morning, it is clear to Henry that war, injury, and even death are not the end. The rising sun turns the icy river to silver and the windows of the Longfellow home to gold.

Henry's children, bundled in winter wool, are whisked past snowy fields, through wooded hills and valleys, along the road to home. They look up, blinking and giggling in the falling snow. And they hear the sounds that make Christmas . . . *Christmas*.

They hear the bells!

From his desk, Henry hears them, too. Renewed, he plunges his pen into fresh ink, joyfully drawing it across a sheet of snow white paper . . .

I heard the bells on Christmas day
Their old familiar carols play,
And wild and sweet the words repeat
Of peace on earth, good will to men.

In those bells the message is clear: On Christmas day a Child was born in a stable. Of that Child, Henry writes: "Though in a manger Thou draw breath, Thou art greater than Life and Death."
And so He is!

Then pealed the bells more loud and deep:
"God is not dead, nor doth he sleep;
The wrong shall fail, the right prevail,
With peace on earth, good will to men."

As the bells ring on, Henry dips his pen again and again. Because Christmas lives on, Fanny lives on, Charles lives on, a nation lives on, and we—each one of us—may live on as well, in hope and peace forever.

Till, ringing, singing, on its way,
The world revolved from night to day,
A voice, a chime, a chant sublime,
Of peace on earth, good will to men!
Good will to men!

IN THE DARK STREETS SHINETH

A 1941 Christmas Eve Story

NARRATED BY DAVID MCCULLOUGH

Music is a part of our history. It is an expression of who we are and the times we've known, our highs, our lows, and so much that we love. Take away American music from the American story and you take away a good part of the soul of the story.

Impossible to imagine life in America without it—without "Shenandoah," or "Amazing Grace," or "The Battle Hymn of the Republic." Or Gershwin or Copland or Scott Joplin. Or the music of Christmas in America.

I would like to tell you the story of two classic American Christmas carols—two of my favorites—that both figured in one of the darkest times ever, during the Second World War.

Shortly before Christmas 1941, Prime Minister Winston Churchill, at considerable personal risk, crossed the Atlantic in great secrecy to meet with President Franklin D. Roosevelt.

On Christmas Eve, from a balcony at the White House, the two leaders spoke to a crowd of 20,000 gathered in the twilight. As reported in the *Washington Post*, "A crescent moon hung overhead. To the southward loomed the Washington Monument . . . as the sun dipped . . . behind the Virginia hills."

President Roosevelt pressed a button to light the Christmas tree. Then he spoke to the crowd, and by radio the world was listening.

"Our strongest weapon in this war," he said, "is that conviction of the dignity and brotherhood of man which Christmas Day signifies."

Churchill began his remarks. Here he was, he said, far from his own country, far from his family. "Yet I cannot truthfully say that I feel far from home," he told the hushed throng.

"Here, in the midst of war, raging and roaring over all the lands and seas, creeping nearer to our hearts and homes, here, amid all the tumult, we have tonight the peace of the spirit in each cottage home and in every generous heart. . . . Here, then, for one night only, each home . . . should be a brightly-lighted island of happiness and peace."

The following morning, Christmas Day, the Prime Minister and the President went to church, where with the congregation they joined in singing "O Little Town of Bethlehem," which Churchill had never heard before.

The words of the hymn, one of the most beloved of Christmas carols, had been written long before by a famous American clergyman, Phillips Brooks, after a visit to the Holy Land.

On Christmas Eve in Jerusalem in 1865, Brooks rode through the dark by horseback to the place above the town where, he was told, the shepherds had gathered with their sheep.

After returning to his church in Philadelphia, in an effort to put down on paper what he had felt that night, Brooks wrote a poem.

A few days before Christmas 1868, he asked the organist, Lewis Redner, to put the poem to music, that it might be sung at the Christmas service.

Redner tried but with no success. He went to bed Christmas Eve feeling he had utterly failed. "My brain was all confused," he later said. "But I was roused from sleep late in the night hearing an angel-strain . . . and seizing a piece of music paper I jotted down the treble of the tune."

Churchill had spoken in his remarks from the White House balcony of every home as a "brightly-lighted island" in the dark. In the first stanza of "O Little Town of Bethlehem" is the line, "Yet in thy dark streets shineth the everlasting Light."

I like to think of Churchill and Roosevelt singing that line in particular. And, as would be said of the Prime Minister, he always sang lustily, if not exactly in tune.

By 1942, with the war still raging, more than 1,000,000 Americans were serving overseas, in sixty-five parts of the world, and it was with those men and women and their families in mind that two talented New Yorkers, lyricist Kim Gannon and composer Walter Kent, went to work on a new Christmas song.

Walter Kent had already composed "The White Cliffs of Dover," which had become nearly an anthem in Britain. Now they wrote "I'll Be Home for Christmas," which in simplest terms expressed the longing for home and light in the darkness felt by so many.

When recorded by Bing Crosby in 1943, the song became the most popular carol of the era, even more than "White Christmas."

History can be a great source of strength and affirmation, and especially in difficult, dangerous times. And the words and music we love, and that have stood the test of time, mean still more when we know their story.

Franklin D. Roosevelt Christmas Eve Message, 1941

Fellow workers for freedom:

There are many men and women in America—sincere and faithful men and women—who are asking themselves this Christmas:

How can we light our trees? How can we give our gifts? How can we meet and worship with love and with uplifted spirit and heart in a world at war, a world of fighting and suffering and death?

How can we pause, even for a day, even for Christmas Day, in our urgent labor of arming a decent humanity against the enemies which beset it?

How can we put the world aside, as men and women put the world aside in peaceful years, to rejoice in the birth of Christ?

These are natural—inevitable—questions in every part of the world which is resisting the evil thing.

And even as we ask these questions, we know the answer. There is another preparation demanded of this nation beyond and beside the preparation of weapons and materials of war. There is demanded also of us the preparation of our hearts; the arming of our hearts. And when we make ready our hearts for the labor and the suffering and the ultimate victory which lie ahead, then we observe Christmas Day—with all of its memories and all of its meanings—as we should.

Looking into the days to come, I have set aside a Day of Prayer, and in that Proclamation I have said:

"The year 1941 has brought upon our nation a war of aggression by powers dominated by arrogant rulers whose selfish purpose is to destroy free institutions. They would thereby take from the freedom-loving peoples of the earth the hard-won liberties gained over many centuries.

"The new year of 1942 calls for the courage and the resolution of old and young to help to win a world struggle in order that we may preserve all that we hold dear.

"We are confident in our devotion to country, in our love of freedom, in our inheritance of courage. But our strength, as the strength of all men everywhere, is of greater avail as God upholds us.

"Therefore, I . . . do hereby appoint the first day of the year 1942 as a day of prayer, of asking forgiveness for our shortcomings of the past, of consecration to the tasks of the present, of asking God's help in days to come.

"We need His guidance that this people may be humble in spirit but strong in the

conviction of the right; steadfast to endure sacrifice, and brave to achieve a victory of liberty and peace."

Our strongest weapon in this war is that conviction of the dignity and brotherhood of man which Christmas Day signifies—more than any other day or any other symbol.

Against enemies who preach the principles of hate and practice them, we set our faith in human love and in God's care for us and all men everywhere.

It is in that spirit, and with particular thoughtfulness of those, our sons and brothers, who serve in our armed forces on land and sea, near and far—those who serve for us and endure for us—that we light our Christmas candles now across the continent from one coast to the other on this Christmas Eve.

We have joined with many other nations and peoples in a very great cause. Millions of them have been engaged in the task of defending good with their life-blood for months and for years.

One of their great leaders stands beside me. He and his people in many parts of the world are having their Christmas trees with their little children around them, just as we do here. He and his people have pointed the way in courage and in sacrifice for the sake of little children everywhere.

And so I am asking my associate, my old and good friend, to say a word to the people of America, old and young, tonight—Winston Churchill, Prime Minister of Great Britain.

Winston Churchill Christmas Eve Message, 1941

I spend this anniversary and festival far from my country, far from my family, yet I cannot truthfully say that I feel far from home. Whether it be the ties of blood on my mother's side, or the friendships I have developed here over many years of active life, or the commanding sentiment of comradeship in the common cause of great peoples who speak the same language, who kneel at the same altars, and to a very large extent, pursue the same ideals, I cannot feel myself a stranger here in the centre and at the summit of the United States. I feel a sense of unity and fraternal association which, added to the kindliness of your welcome, convinces me that I have a right to sit at your fireside and share your Christmas joys.

This is a strange Christmas Eve. Almost the whole world is locked in deadly struggle, and, with the most terrible weapons which science can devise, the nations advance upon each other. Ill would it be for us this Christmastide if we were not sure that no greed for the land or wealth of any other people, no vulgar ambition, no morbid lust for material gain at the expense of others, had led us to the field. Here, in the midst of war, raging and roaring over all the lands and seas, creeping nearer to our hearts and homes, here, amid all the tumult, we have tonight the peace of the spirit in each cottage home and in every generous heart. Therefore we may cast aside for this night at least the cares and dangers which beset us, and make for the children an evening of happiness in a world of storm.

Here, then, for one night only, each home throughout the English-speaking world should be a brightly-lighted island of happiness and peace.

Let the children have their night of fun and laughter. Let the gifts of Father Christmas delight their play. Let us grown-ups share to the full in their unstinted pleasures before we turn again to the stern task and the formidable years that lie before us, resolved that, by our sacrifice and daring, these same children shall not be robbed of their inheritance or denied their right to live in a free and decent world.

And so, in God's mercy, a happy Christmas to you all.

SING, CHOIRS OF ANGELS!

The Beginnings of The Tabernacle Choir

NARRATED BY MICHAEL YORK

To tell a true story truly, one must always begin in the middle.

For example, at Christmas, we tell of shepherds keeping watch over their flocks by night. But that was not the shepherds' first night in the field! They had been on those hills for generations, learning from their fathers and teaching their sons. And surely, the Wise Men who came from the East had parents. And even the angels, whose songs filled the heavens, had friends.

None of us begin and end with ourselves. None of our stories are ours alone. As with all stories of Christmas—of gifts and of giving—the story of one is the story of all. Which is to say that *this* true story is *your* story too!

And so, we begin . . . in the middle.

On a winter night—in 1789, to be exact—the village of New Market in North Wales, not far from where my own father was born, was dark and quiet under the wide, white blanket of winter. Yet one house was ablaze with the joy of Christmas. A healthy boy had been born to Bernard and Elizabeth Parry. In recent years, two of their children had died within four days of each other.

But this night, the sorrow of that loss was lifted. Bernard took the infant in his arms and echoed the words of the angel who had visited Zacharias. "His name will be John," he pronounced. "John Parry," as if the name itself held the promise of endless life and future greatness. "So, sleep, my child. Sleep!"

Sleep, my child, and peace attend thee,
All through the night.
Guardian angels God will send thee,
All through the night.

If that was the child's first lullaby, it serves to introduce his story. John's gift would be music and singing. And guardian angels, including his departed family members, seemed to shape his life's song.

John grew up freely running through the hills and green valleys of Wales, his soul overflowing with music. As the people of Wales say, "To be born Welsh is to be born privileged. Not with a silver spoon in your mouth, but with music in your blood and poetry in your soul."

Inheriting the gifts of his father, John became a singer, a poet, and a composer. He learned to play the harp and the flute. He also learned the family trade: the art of masonry—of fitting uwieldy stones together to make them as one. Whether joining stones, poetic words, or voices in song, John learned to build things that would last.

When John was sixteen, his mother died. But she was never far from him. Her angelic melodies were already woven through the music of his life.

> *The ash grove how graceful, how plainly 'tis speaking*
> *The wind through it playing has language for me.*
> *Whenever the light through its branches is breaking,*
> *A host of kind faces is gazing on me.*

At nineteen, John wed Mary Williams. They raised seven children. As with most families of their day, some of those children died. But John and Mary never felt entirely without them.

Whenever music filled John's soul, all his children seemed to be near.

During those years, he became a preacher. In time, a religious movement on the other side of the Atlantic beckoned him. With few earthly belongings but laden with heavenly gifts, John and Mary joined 249 of their countrymen and boarded a ship bound for America.

Out on the open sea, John organized other Welsh passengers into a choir. Singing knit their hearts together and bolstered their faith. And how they would need that faith! After landing and beginning their long trek west, one in every five immigrants died of cholera. John's wife, Mary, contracted the disease, and she succumbed as well. John was heartbroken. Yet, in his sorrow, life's music poured even more deeply from his soul.

John's little Welsh choir pushed on, singing as they crossed the western plains. Along the trail, travelers from other nations put their heads out of their wagons to hear the music. Some would come running just to be near the singers. When asked where their choir had learned to sing and who had taught them, one traveler recorded, "The hills of Wales were their schoolhouse and the Spirit of God was their teacher."

That Spirit was felt whenever they sang the words of their countryman—words they knew by heart:

> *Guide us, O Thou great Jehovah,*
> *Guide us to the promised land.*
> *We are weak, but Thou art able;*
> *Hold us with thy pow'rful hand.*
> *Holy Spirit, Holy Spirit,*
> *Feed us till the Savior comes,*
> *Feed us till the Savior comes.*

When the choir finally arrived in the great valley, their reputation had gone before them. They were invited to sing in meetings and at celebrations. Though few in number, their Welsh traditions gave them strength, and their unity gave them power.

Soon, the governor of the territory invited John to organize and conduct a new choir. The fledgling ensemble would be named after a great domed edifice soon to be built. The Tabernacle Choir was born.

But, not precisely. The story of The Tabernacle Choir does not begin or end with itself. Just look into the faces of the Choir members. In the light of their eyes you can find the spirit and gifts of John Parry and the little Welsh choir that came West.

But that is the middle of the story. There is much, much more. The gifts of their fathers and mothers, grandparents and children are there also. Even hearing the Choir, we feel the presence of our ancestors before us and generations after. And each Christmas, when snow flies and the wide mountain valley is blanketed in white, the story of the Choir becomes the story of us all. It is the story of giving our gifts—of giving ourselves—whenever we are joined in song.

Sing, choirs of angels, sing in exultation,
Sing, all ye citizens of heaven above.

O come let us adore Him,
O come let us adore Him
O come let us adore Him,
Christ, the Lord!

This, then, is the true story of the Tabernacle Choir. Song by song, soul by soul, what John Parry helped to build does indeed last. With shepherds, Wise Men, and the angels, we are one. So, sing, choirs of angels! And with your exultations, we joyfully sing with you!

Yea, Lord, we greet thee, born this happy morning;
Jesus, to thee be glory given!
Son of the Father, now in flesh appearing!

O come let us adore Him,
O come let us adore Him,
O come let us adore Him,
Christ, the Lord!

GOOD KING WENCESLAS

The Hidden Parable in the Familiar Carol

NARRATED BY JANE SEYMOUR

The castle was brimming with the blessings of Christmas—not just because festive music rang through the corridors and pine boughs trimmed every beam.

On this St. Stephen's Day, the courtiers had gathered their Christmas treasures and given them to the poor. Now, as the Feast of St. Stephen drew to a close, seventy knights pushed back long wooden tables and offered their hands. Seventy noble women lifted the edges of their gowns and glided to meet them.

Bathed in the glow of a well-fed fire, King Wenceslas looked out upon his court and, at the signal of his benevolent smile, their Christmas revelry began.

With a nod to his page, King Wenceslas slipped behind the throne into the darkness of his private chamber. The page boy was hungry and weary from waiting. "Now can we eat?" he complained, sliding to the floor.

"In time," the king answered, turning away. The king had cared for the boy since his childhood, and soon the boy would be a man. With a wave of sadness, he realized that the blessings of Christmas had already come to his courtiers, but not yet to his loyal page. Was it too late? he wondered.

From a tall, narrow window, King Wenceslas watched the sun hang on crimson clouds and die away. He studied the hedge-bound fields and rolling hills, now swallowed up in snow. His eyes narrowed. There, against a row of spidery trees, was a dark speck—a man, perhaps, stooping and searching for wood to warm his family.

Good King Wenceslas looked out
On the feast of Stephen,
When the snow lay round about,
Deep and crisp and even;

Brightly shone the moon that night,
Though the frost was cruel,
When a poor man came in sight,
Gathering winter fuel.

"Come quickly, lad!" he called. As the boy struggled to his feet, King Wenceslas seized his hand and dashed up narrow steps to a turret balcony. "Look! Do you see him?" The king pointed, breathlessly.

For a moment, the page boy could not speak. Rarely had he seen the world in quite this way—asleep under a coverlet of white, glistening under a full moon. The boy would have fallen asleep himself but for the wonder that was waking within him.

When the dark figure moved again, the king guided the boy's gaze. "There, in the trees! Do you see him now?"

"Yes, yes," the boy answered.

"And?" pressed the king. "Is he one of the household? Is he one of us?"

"Oh, no, sire," said the boy. "None of us would be out there, what with the freezing cold, and heaven only knows what creatures might be lurking!"

"Hither, page, and stand by me,
If thou know'st it, telling,
Yonder peasant, who is he?
Where and what his dwelling?"

"Sire, he lives a good league hence,
Underneath the mountain,
Right against the forest fence,
By St. Agnes fountain."

King Wenceslas took comfort that the boy knew the people of the kingdom—even those who lived far from the castle. And he rejoiced that the humble peasant, foraging in the snow, could very well be the boy's salvation.

As before, the king snatched the page boy's hand and led him down a winding staircase. "Down, down is the way," the king mused to himself as they hurried along.

In the royal pantry, he tossed the page a satchel and ordered him to fill it. As they worked, the page noticed the king's eyes were wet, though his speaking was giddy, like laughter. "Hurry, my boy! Hurry!"

> *"Bring me flesh and fruit so fine,*
> *Bring me pine logs hither,*
> *Thou and I will see him dine,*
> *When we bear them thither."*
>
> *Page and monarch forth they went,*
> *Forth they went together,*
> *Through the rude wind's wild lament*
> *And the bitter weather.*

Soon the king and his page boy were following the peasant's tracks. King Wenceslas carried a cord of split logs across his strong shoulders, wrapped tightly to keep them dry, and in each hand he clutched a heavy cloth sack. Behind him, the page boy bravely struggled under the weight of his own satchel.

The boy wondered if he ought to watch for creatures lurking in the shadows, but in his heart he knew there were none. Indeed, looking into the infinite expanse above, he saw snowflakes descending like concourses of angels, winging their way down to watch over him and lead him safely along.

As the sky cleared, the night air grew colder. The soft blanket of snow that had first enticed the boy now threatened to ensnare him. With every step, its icy surface broke

into shards, trapping the boy's feet and turning them to ice. When the boy could no longer feel his toes, he pled with the king for rest and relief.

> *"Sire, the night is darker now*
> *And the wind grows stronger;*
> *Fails my heart I know not how;*
> *I can go no longer."*

King Wenceslas answered tenderly, as one walking the same path himself.

> *"Mark my footsteps good, my page;*
> *Tread thou in them boldly;*
> *Thou shalt find the winter's rage*
> *Freeze thy blood less coldly."*

It was a strange invitation—to walk in the king's footsteps. At first the boy struggled to do it. But as before, Wenceslas took his hand and helped him find the path. Soon the boy was marching boldly behind his master. Miraculously, with each step, his frozen feet began to warm, and the warmth rose within him and gave him strength.

In his master's steps he trod
Where the snow lay dinted;
Heat was in the very sod
Which the saint had printed.

Therefore, Christians, all be sure,
Wealth or rank possessing,
Ye who now will bless the poor,
Shall yourselves find blessing.

At the edge of the dark forest, a little cottage came into view, its golden light sparkling on the surface of an icebound spring. With a single knock, the king and his page boy were welcomed into the circle of a large and happy family. As guests in the house, they were invited to rest, but the boy would not be still. With the children as his helpers, he fed the fire and set out the unexpected meal. When all had feasted to fatness, they pushed the little table back and began to sing and dance.

From the corner of the cottage, good King Wenceslas watched the boy dance, and smiled to himself. The boy was taking the hands of the children and leading each one, just as he had been led. Their sweet, innocent laughter was the music of Christmas, filling the room and ringing through the forest.

In time, the king and his page boy reluctantly left the warm cottage and ventured once more across the snowy fields. Side by side they strode, now heedless of the cold night air. And the king knew that it was not too late. Now the blessings of Christmas had come to all of his kingdom, because they had come to the boy.

Therefore, Christians, all be sure,
Wealth or rank possessing,
Ye who now will bless the poor,
Shall yourselves find blessing.

CHRISTMAS FROM HEAVEN

The True Story of the Berlin Candy Bomber

NARRATED BY TOM BROKAW

O n Christmas Eve, 1948, somewhere between Wiesbaden and Berlin, a twenty-seven-year-old American pilot gazed into the night sky.

The heavens were so full of stars, it seemed they would overflow and tumble to earth in a brilliant display of Christmas generosity and joy.

Hal, as he was known to his crew, wrapped his hands around the yoke of his C-54 cargo plane packed with 20,000 pounds of flour. "This is the real spirit of Christmas," he thought to himself as he guided his plane toward Tempelhof Air Base in West Berlin.

When World War II had ended three years earlier, Germany and its capital city were divided between the Western allies and the Soviet Union. Then, in a grab for power, Stalin blocked ground transportation into the city. To preserve freedom and keep two and a half million West Berliners from starving, the United States and Great Britain began transporting food and other basic supplies by air. Hal was one of hundreds of Americans who participated in the historic Berlin Airlift, which was called "Operation Vittles."

That snowy Christmas Eve, as Hal radioed for clearance to land, his mind wandered back six months to the day that had changed his life. He had been standing at the end of the Tempelhof runway, taking home movies of arriving planes, when he noticed about thirty children on a grassy strip just beyond a barbed wire fence. In broken English, they asked about the planes, how much flour each one carried, and whether the airlift would continue. Although the children had been on meager rations, they were more concerned with freedom than with flour. They wanted what Hal had always had—the opportunity to pursue their dreams.

For nearly an hour Hal answered their questions before saying good-bye. As he turned away, one question lingered in his mind: "What makes these kids different?" All over the world, children were known to beg candy from American servicemen. These children had little to eat, and no candy at all, yet they were grateful for what the airlift had given them and asked for nothing. Their gratitude melted Hal's heart.

Instinctively he wanted to give something back. Digging into his pockets, he found only two sticks of gum. "From little things come big things," his father used to say. A broad smile crossed Hal's boyish face. Giving so little to so many could cause a squabble, he reasoned. But a quiet voice within him urged him on.

So, Hal broke the gum into four pieces and passed it through the fence.

Without a word, the four children tore the gum wrappers into strips and passed them to the others. One by one, each small nose was pressed to the paper, breathing in the minty smell. Never had he seen such expressions of joy and wonder, even at Christmas.

As Hal watched in amazement, his mind raced. "If only I had more to give!" he thought. He had his own rations of gum and chocolate. Maybe his buddies would be willing to donate theirs. Just then another C-54 roared over his head and an idea formed in his mind. "I could drop candy from the air," he said to himself.

He quickly explained his plan to the children. When they asked how to recognize his plane, he remembered flying over the family farm back home.

"I'll wiggle my wings," he announced, spreading his long arms and waving them up and down. The children giggled with delight. "Just promise me you'll share the candy," he said. All heads nodded in agreement.

By the next day, Hal had secretly enlisted his crew to donate their rations and make parachutes from handkerchiefs.

As Hal's plane approached the runway and the grass came into view, he wiggled his wings, and a knot of waiting children exploded, running and jumping in the air. With the precision of bombardiers, the airmen pushed the candy out the flare chute, and white canopies floated to earth. Thirty children ran with open arms to catch the treasures.

Hal and his buddies were as excited as the children. The thrill of giving was irresistible. Soon they were dropping parachutes every day—hundreds of them.

The press caught on, and reports went out. Mail for "Uncle Wiggly Wings" began piling up at Base Operations. Hal found himself standing before his superior, expecting to be court-martialed. But the colonel surprised him. "Halvorsen," he said, "General Tunner thinks it's a good idea."

Soon hundreds of airmen were donating rations. Operation Little Vittles quickly captured the imagination of people everywhere. Candy and handkerchiefs poured in from around the world. Hal became known as "The Candy Bomber" and "The Chocolate Pilot."

Across West Berlin, children gathered to catch the parachutes and share the candy with each other. And they sent hundreds of thank-you letters, like the one addressed to "Dear Onkl of the Heaven." Some included maps and instructions: "Fly along the big canal to the second bridge, turn right one block. I live in the bombed-out house on the corner. I'll be in the backyard every day at 2 p.m. Drop the chocolate there."

Day by day, the parachutes brought peace and the candy renewed hope. The children made friends of their former enemies, and their parents' hearts were softened. The wounds of war began to heal.

By December, the Little Vittles operation had gathered eighteen tons of candy from American candy makers, and three more tons came in from private donors. The spirit of Christmas was descending on people everywhere, lifting them up in the joy of giving.

That Christmas Eve, the twenty-seven-year-old American pilot blinked back tears. The stars overhead could not be more beautiful than skies overflowing with parachutes, tumbling to earth in a brilliant display of Christmas generosity and joy.

His father was right: "From little things come big things." Hal in his cockpit pulled back on the yoke as his wheels rolled onto the familiar runway. This is the real spirit of Christmas—to give whatever we have, no matter how small the gift.

In that moment Hal Halvorsen prayed for the courage to never give anything less.

GOD BLESS US, EVERY ONE!

Imagining How Dickens's Carol *Came to Be*

NARRATED BY JOHN RHYS-DAVIES

One hundred and seventy years ago, Charles Dickens wrote a little book immortalizing the holiday we know and love as Christmas. But the story of how that book came to be is as interesting as the book itself. Step back to 1843. It was, to borrow Dickens's own words, "the worst of times."

Dickens was in his prime: average height, smooth faced, looking as he did before the beard and unruly hair you've seen in pictures. At thirty-one, he was already the most successful and best-loved novelist of his day. But installments of his current novel weren't selling as expected, and his publisher, Mr. Chapman, was nervous.

"I don't understand!" Dickens protested.

Mr. Chapman peered over his spectacles and drew a long breath. "Mr. Dickens, let me be clear. If people don't start buying your books, we'll have to reduce your weekly advance."

Dickens couldn't believe his ears. "But this is my finest work!" he declared.

There were other troubles as well. For years, Dickens had used his money to support worthy causes and needy family members. "Oh, come now, Charlie," his younger brother Alfred would cajole, "what's twenty pounds to you? You have more money than you will ever need!"

But Dickens knew better. "Alfred, our situation is desperate," he explained. "Soon we'll have nothing left."

To make matters worse, Dickens's wife, Catherine, was expecting a baby. "Charles," she lamented, "we will soon have our fifth child! Can we not have even the semblance of a proper nursery?"

"Kate, dear, try to understand," Dickens pled. "In three months we may not have even the semblance of a proper house!" With a heavy mortgage, mounting bills, and the cost of maintaining his public presence, the celebrated author was on the brink of bankruptcy. "Oh, my love," he implored, drawing Kate close, imagining the worst. "What will become of us? What will become of our children?"

That autumn, Dickens walked the streets of London. Night after night, mile after mile, he looked into the faces of London's poor and saw the specter of what might be.

"Alms! Alms!" begged a pallid child.

"Watch it, Mister!" growled an angry factory worker.

A Cockney maiden plied her feminine wiles. "Ooooh, it's a proper gentleman!" she purred.

A student leapt in Dickens's path and shoved out his hand. "Spare a bob, sir?"

Passing dingy basement windows caked with soot, Dickens was haunted by a memory from his own impoverished childhood. The terrifying scene of his father's arrest played itself out again and again in his mind:

"John Dickens!" barked the constable.

"Yes?" answered Dickens's father.

"Come with me!"

"But sir, my children—"

The officer pointed his billy club menacingly, pushing facts in his father's face. "Thems that put themselves in debtors' prison due to fraud and foolishness agree, by their own course of action, to have their children remanded to the public workhouse."

Dickens could still hear his mother's voice crying out, "No, John! No!" while little Alfred begged in vain, "Papa, Papa! Don't go!"

Nevertheless, his father was dragged off to debtors' prison, and twelve-year-old Charles was taken from school and forced to labor in the dismal dungeon of a boot-blacking factory.

Shrinking from his father's fate, Dickens closed his heart, his mind, and his purse. He walked the narrow alleyways and empty park lanes alone, depressed, his hands in his pockets. His mind worked on his problem as his problem worked on him.

"What could I write quickly?" he wondered to himself. "A brief tale . . . one volume . . . finished in time for a holiday gift? Yes! Let me see . . ."

With each step, an idea took shape in Dickens's mind: the story of a man so preoccupied with money that he cannot appreciate the joy of family and friends—a man so fearful of ignorance and want that he cannot embrace the abundant beauties around him. Why not bring all of this to life? Emboldened by his plan, Dickens sequestered himself in his study and began to write.

"The central character—a tight-fisted, hand-at-the-grindstone Scrooge . . ." As he wrote, he could hear the old man's grasping, stingy voice. "Bah, humbug!"

Dickens continued scribbling. "With a dead business partner who regrets his own miserly ways, Jacob Marley." Again a hollow voice reverberated: "I wear the chain I forged in life!"

As the story flowed from Dickens's pen, the characters came to life in his mind. "A clerk, Bob Cratchit; his family; their sickly son, Tiny Tim; Scrooge's nephew; and a myriad of debtors—all of them suffering because Scrooge sees only himself!"

Now, how to give Scrooge a new vision of his life and the people around him—a vision that will change his heart? He would need a helper, a guide. Dickens provided one by reviving a character he had originally created for another story—a ghost, though far from ghoulish. Dickens described him as a jolly giant with a genial face, sparkling eye, open hand, and joyful air. As the story unfolded, that ghost would have much to say about Dickens's own troubles.

What does an author learn from the characters he is inventing? How might a genial ghost change the way Charles Dickens sees the world? What happened as Dickens brought his ghost to life we can only imagine—but what a story imagination tells!

"Charles!" boomed a cheery baritone voice, shattering the quiet of Dickens's mind. There in his study was an enormous man of unconstrained demeanor, dressed in a simple green robe and wearing a wreath of holly on his head.

"Whaaaa?! What is it? Who are you?"

"Come in! Come in, and know me better, man! I am the Ghost of Christmas Present."

Instinctively, Dickens reached for his notebook. "Yes, let me get this down."

"Put that away," the ghost chided. "Look at yourself. Day after day you hold on to your pen, clutching tightly to the world as you know it, afraid to leave it behind for something better."

"Afraid?" Dickens sputtered, as if it could never be true.

"Yes!" declared the ghost. "And yet here you are, approaching the season when hope and abundance should fill your heart."

"You mean Christmas!" said Dickens.

"Indeed! At least you've not forgotten that!"

Charles tried to defend himself. "But I have always seen Christmas as a wonder, sir, with all its merriment and whatnot."

"You haven't seen anything!" thundered the ghost.

"I haven't?"

"No, you haven't! Look out there!"

Dickens strained his eyes. "What? I can't see anything!"

"Of course you can't! From where you are, there's nothing to see but yourself! Here, take hold of my robe. Come on. A little breeze now, and up we go!"

Suddenly Dickens felt his toes lifting from the floor, the walls of his room vanishing around him.

"Aghhhh!" he cried out like a child tossed in the air and caught again, unsure whether to be frightened or delighted.

The ghost had seen this a thousand times before, yet he never tired of it. "Yes, yes!" he erupted with joy. "This is the wonder—seeing things as they really are!"

Indeed. Dickens could hardly catch his breath. "Look! Look at the city from here!"

"And what do you see, my good man?"

Dickens was dumbfounded by the obvious. "I . . . I see houses and houses—so many houses!"

"Because there are so many people," explained the ghost.

Dickens's mind caught hold upon a thought. "People, yes . . . and all of them buying books!"

"It's not about books!" the ghost exploded. "See the people, Charles, with their own lives."

"Lives?" Dickens asked.

"Yes, and their own troubles—like you."

"Ahh! I see!"

But the ghost was firm. "Not yet, you don't. But you will!"

Dropping through a cloud, they saw the city stretched out before them, candles in windows and streetlamps mapping the maze of narrow lanes. "Look at the lights!" Dickens called to his companion.

"Yes!"

"And the river!" Dickens was becoming expert at identifying the world from above.

"Oh, yes!" said the ghost.

"And the Houses of Parliament, Big Ben, and the Abbey!"

"Yes, much is familiar!" assured the ghost. "But come, what haven't you seen before?"

They flew north across a quilt of woolly white, its irregular patches stitched together by ancient dry stone walls. The brilliant moon made silvery ribbons of the rivers and diamonds of every frozen pond. A layer of snow upon the rooftops tucked the world in for a dreamy sleep, and nothing could awaken it.

"It's all so very still," Dickens whispered.

"Yes."

"And beautiful."

"Indeed! Now, look there, Charles—out upon the moor, where nothing grows but moss and furze and coarse rank grass."

Dickens's eyes traced the outline of high, wide hills and the shadows of deep-cut valleys. A single speck of firelight flickered in the distance. "It's a place where miners live, who labor in the bowels of the earth."

"And yet, in all their want, they know me—they know Christmas!"

"They do?" It hadn't occurred to Dickens that the Christmas he had always loved could be found here, too.

The ghost guided Dickens's eyes. "Look! A cheerful company is assembled round the fire: an old, old man and woman with their children and their children's children, all decked out gaily in their best attire, singing a Christmas carol. Their voices rise above the howling of the wind upon the barren waste."

Aye, and therefore be you merry;
Rejoice and be merry;
Set sorrows aside!
Christ Jesus, our Savior,
Was born on this tide.

Dickens was transfixed by their joyful singing in such humble circumstances. "They are so poor. They haven't anything at all but each other!"

"It's true," said the ghost, pleased that Dickens was beginning to understand. "Now go, Charles. Fly on!" the ghost urged. "There is more you must see, and see for *yourself*!"

Dickens passed above the moor and flew toward the sea. He looked back and saw the last of the land. Ahead, a dismal reef of sunken rocks a league or so from shore came into view. "Look!" shouted the ghost above the thundering water, roaring and raging among the dreadful caverns it had worn.

"A lighthouse!" Dickens exclaimed.

"Yes. See within the loophole of the thick stone wall—that ray of brightness on this awful sea?"

Dickens hovered close. "I see a man and his wife, their hands rough, faces scarred from hard weather. They too sing a carol, like a gale in itself."

"Yes, yes!" cried the ghost, anxious for Dickens to hear. "And what is their joyful song?"

I saw three ships come sailing in
On Christmas Day, on Christmas Day;
I saw three ships come sailing in
On Christmas Day in the morning.

Dickens studied the unlikely scene. "How happy they seem to be!"

The ghost was encouraged. "Ah, now you're getting a glimpse of it! On you go, across the black and heaving sea—far away from any shore."

Dickens and the ghost sped on. Far off in the distance, a dark form sat quietly in the moonlight. "Ahh! A ship!" Dickens observed.

The ghost nudged him closer. "See the helmsman at the wheel, the lookout in the bow, the officers on the watch."

As Dickens lighted on the deck, he observed, "Every man among them hums a Christmas carol or has a Christmas thought."

To which the ghost added, "And speaks below his breath of Christmas, with homeward hopes. And every man on board has a kinder word today than any other day."

Dickens struggled to make sense of it all. "It's Christmas—even out here. It's Christmas in their hearts. And that's enough for them."

But the ghost would not let Dickens linger. "Yes! Now on!" he cried as they soared over rolling hills and rivers toward home. Charles could not help pointing out the beauty of the city he knew so well. "Ah! London! The Marble Arch! Kensington Gardens! The Thames!"

Soon they were slowing and then hovering over a large, brick building bordered with high walls and heavy iron gates. It was much like the factory where young Dickens had been forced to support his family. "What do you see, Charles?" implored the ghost. "What do you *really* see?"

Charles looked down. "Uggghh!" he cried, averting his eyes. "An orphanage, a workhouse yard, with so many poor, miserable orphans, so pitiful in their—"

But the sound of sweet, melodious voices stopped him, leaving him speechless. "What?!" he cried, disbelieving. "They're singing!"

> *The first Noel the angel did say*
> *Was to certain poor shepherds in fields as they lay.*

Dickens could hardly comprehend it.

"In their wretched condition—singing!"

"Yes, Charles. Even them."

As the wind rose, the ghost drew Dickens up. "Come now, Charles, see everyone."

"See? Oh, I do!" Dickens replied confidently. "It's my business to see, you know, and to write about it! Like that young man there, with such great expectations! And the little seamstress. And the lame boy. And look there, that gentleman, walking in the street."

The ghost paused. "What about him?"

Dickens answered as if describing another character. "Alone, hands in his pockets, head bowed low. He's not singing, I can tell you!"

But the ghost pressed Dickens, "Look again! Look closely, Charles!"

Dickens gasped. "Ohhh! No! No, it can't be," he cried in disbelief. "It's me!"

"It is. And what are you doing down there?" the ghost asked.

"I'm walking, scheming, plotting . . . convincing myself that money will solve my problems, that publishing a little Christmas book will relieve my woe."

"And can it?"

"Not finally, not forever. . . . But you can. You have!"

"I have?" the ghost asked knowingly.

"Yes. Christmas should be kept here, now, in the present and always. Good Spirit, I see! I do see!"

"Come, then," said the happy ghost. "It is time to go home."

As they flew, Dickens declared his resolution. "I will do more than merely write of

Scrooge, Cratchit, and Tiny Tim. I will learn what they learn, and live it! I will honor Christmas in my heart and try to keep it all the year!"

Suddenly they were back in Dickens's library, the half-finished manuscript still on the desk. Dickens turned to the ghost. "Sir, I cannot thank you enough. It's not too late for Scrooge, and it's not too late for me."

"Indeed, it is not. But I'd best be off now. You have a little book to finish."

"Yes, yes! And you'll be in it!"

The smiling visage of the ghost shimmered as he slowly disappeared in the first golden light of morning.

We cannot say what imaginary encounter Dickens may have enjoyed with the ghost he invented. But that autumn of 1843, something happened as Dickens dipped his pen and filled his paper. His little story—which he had intended as a means to reclaim his wealth—turned out to be the instrument for recovering his faith in others and hope in the future. Each morning he awoke eager to begin the day's work, filling his story with the Christmas spirit he had discovered anew. He poured all of his experience—all of himself—into the writing.

Dickens later wrote to a friend, "I was reluctant to lay the manuscript aside even for a moment. I wept and laughed and wept again. The spirit of the story captured more than my mind. It took hold of my heart and taught me what I did not know, in a most extraordinary way."

Scrooge and Dickens learned that the spirit of Christmas is the power of love. Dickens captured this spirit perfectly through his depictions of festive family gatherings, dances, games, feasts with all their yuletide trimmings, and of course, Christmas carols. And today, when that spirit is seemingly lost or forgotten, it is "a Dickens Christmas" that helps bring it back in all its wonder and delight. Little surprise that the first edition of *A Christmas Carol* sold out by Christmas Eve and word of its inspiring message spread far and wide.

As Dickens himself recounted, "I received by every post, strangers writing all manner of letters about their homes and hearths and how the Carol is read aloud and kept on a very little shelf all by itself."

Many observed the power of that little book. One writer declared Charles Dickens to be the Apostle of Christmas. Upon Dickens's death, a child was heard to say, "Mr. Dickens dead? Then will Father Christmas die too?" And some have held that if every copy of *A Christmas Carol* were destroyed today, the book could be rewritten tomorrow because so many know the story by heart and recount it every year.

In time, Dickens's fortunes were reversed and he went on to write some of the most notable works of his career. But nothing would equal the literary artifact of his own Christmas awakening. Whether by ghost or no, there on the streets of London, amidst insecurity, fear, and confusion, Charles Dickens discovered the Christmas spirit for himself.

The words of Scrooge's nephew are Dickens's own: "I am sure I have always thought of Christmas time, when it has come round . . . as a good time: a kind, forgiving, charitable, pleasant time: the only time I know of . . . when men and women seem by one consent to open their shutup hearts freely, and to think of people below them as if they really were fellow-passengers to the grave [and beyond]. . . . Though it has never put a scrap of gold or silver in my pocket, I believe that it *has* done me good, and *will* do me good; and I say, God bless it!" To which good people everywhere reply, "God bless us, every one!"

AFTERWORD

Dickens's flight with the Ghost of Christmas Present is pure invention, but the circumstances that led to his writing of *A Christmas Carol* are told in truth. In the fall of 1843, the celebrated author arrived in Manchester to deliver a speech at Athenaeum Hall. His subject—education for the poor—was an expression of a broader theme woven throughout his work. Ironically, poverty had long been a worry for Dickens. As a boy he'd left school to support his family by working in a boot paste factory. Now, earnings from his current novel, *Martin Chuzzlewit,* were down, and his publisher was threatening to discontinue advance payments.

With his wife about to deliver a fifth child, and facing expectations to provide support for loved ones and various other causes, the possibility of financial ruin loomed before him.

Depressed, Dickens walked the streets of Manchester, pondering his predicament. To ease pressure he would need to write something quickly, something likely to sell. On returning to London he continued his late night excursions, working out a simple plot line as he walked.

Along the way he undoubtedly encountered people like the characters he would create: miners, sailors, clerks—ordinary people who were hopelessly poor but genuinely happy. We cannot say whether Dickens's fear of losing his wealth is deliberately reflected in the character of Scrooge, but we can say that his writing of *A Christmas Carol* profoundly influenced Dickens, as it has millions across the world. Through Scrooge's eyes we have been able to look upon our own lives and discover blessings we hadn't perceived before. Time and again, we have been lifted from our sorrows and misfortunes by taking hold of the spirit of Christmas—the power of love—and living more charitably all year through.

FOR UNTO US

The Wondrous Invitation of Handel's Messiah

NARRATED BY MARTIN JARVIS

England, in the late summer of 1741, was not engaged in any great war at home or abroad, but the English people were not at peace. The conflict that rages in the hearts of men and women everywhere—the universal struggle to bear the burdens of mortality including sickness, fear, and injustice—afflicted both rich and poor, enslaved and free.

Those burdens weighed heavily upon George Frideric Handel. For some thirty years, his Italianate operas had delighted audiences—but no more. Handel's most recent opera had closed after only three performances. As the Prince of Prussia declared, "Handel's great days are over, his inspiration is exhausted, and his taste behind the fashion." Indeed, a conflict was raging in Handel's soul.

> *Why do the nations so furiously rage together,*
> *And why do the people imagine a vain thing?*

To sustain himself, Handel had begun composing a different form of musical drama—the oratorio. Often based on familiar stories and sung in English, an oratorio promised to appeal to a broader audience, including those who had rejected Handel's operas.

In June of that year, his librettist Charles Jennens had delivered the text for a new project. "I hope [Handel] will lay out his whole genius and skill upon it," Jennens wrote, "as [this] subject excels every other subject."

The subject for the new oratorio would be the Messiah. In late August, Handel picked up his pen and began composing what would become a 260-page score. But not without a struggle.

Suffering from rheumatism, the paralyzing effects of a stroke, and the psychological burden of enormous personal debt, Handel wrote. Day by day, note by note, he depicted a Messiah who would bear the griefs and sorrows of all people, everywhere, including his own.

> *Surely He hath borne our griefs*
> *And carried our sorrows.*

Twenty-four days later, *Messiah* was completed. By the following April, the new score had been copied, rehearsed, and made ready for its premiere in Dublin, Ireland. It was a charity performance, intended to raise money for people toward whom Handel must have felt particular compassion—those who were hopelessly in debt and incarcerated in debtors' prison. As the tenor soloist stood to sing the first words of the new oratorio, he seemed to be speaking directly to the prisoners and their families:

> *"Comfort ye my people,"*
> *Saith your God.*

A review of the first performance appeared in the *Dublin Journal*: "Words are wanting to express the exquisite delight it afforded to the admiring, crowded audience. The sublime, the grand, and the tender, adapted to the most elevated, majestick and moving words, conspired to transport and charm the ravished heart and ear."

Not only was the oratorio a success, it accomplished its charitable purpose. When the revenue was collected and counted against the debts of the impoverished, 142 prisoners were liberated. Through that first performance of *Messiah*, a price had been paid, prison gates were opened, and the heads of the poor were lifted up in rejoicing. For them, the glory of the Lord had truly been revealed!

> *And the glory of the Lord shall be revealed,*
> *And all flesh shall see it together,*
> *For the mouth of the Lord hath spoken it.*

But success was short-lived. Though *Messiah* was praised in Dublin, it was roundly rejected in London, in part because it was presented at the opera house at Covent Garden. The weekly *Universal Spectator* summed up the general criticism: "An oratorio either is an act of religion, or it is not; if it is, then I ask if the playhouse is a fit temple to perform it in, or a company of players fit ministers of God's word?"

And so, for several years the oratorio was largely ignored. But then Handel arranged for another charity performance—supporting a cause that was familiar to Londoners—and everything changed.

Every day, for many years, destitute women had streamed into the city seeking work as domestic servants. In their desperate state, they were preyed upon by unscrupulous employers, and then, if found to be with child, were callously dismissed by the very men who had used them.

Virtually all women who bore children out of wedlock were shunned by society. As a result, each year hundreds of newborns were abandoned—or worse. As the writer Daniel Defoe observed, "Those who cannot be so hardhearted to murder their own offspring themselves . . . get it done by others, . . . by leaving them to be starved by parish nurses."

The Biblical description of Christ was appropriate for these suffering women and children:

He was despised and rejected,
A man of sorrows and acquainted with grief.

Sometime in the 1720s, a retired English shipwright named Thomas Coram had observed the plight of these women and their babies and began raising money for a "foundling hospital." The purpose of the institution was to adopt the fatherless infants and raise them to lead meaningful lives.

After many years, the new hospital opened its gates under cover of night. More children were brought forward than could possibly be accommodated.

Yet the hospital chapel was still unfinished, and the general committee had depleted its funds. So, Handel, being no stranger to charitable work, made a proposal. As noted in the record: "Mr. Handel . . . generously and charitably offered a performance of vocal and instrumental musick . . . and that the money arising therefrom should be applied to finishing the [hospital] chapel."

And so it was. On the first of May, 1750, *Messiah* was performed in the unfinished chapel—a suitable place for a sacred drama—and proceeds from the concert were used to complete the edifice.

There, in that refuge for the newborn child, Handel helped bring to life the story of the Messiah in a most unusual way. Every nursery became a stable, and every cradle a manger—welcoming hope into the world.

For unto us a child is born, unto us a Son is given:
And the government shall be upon His shoulder,
And His name shall be called
Wonderful, Counsellor,
The Mighty God, the Everlasting Father,
The Prince of Peace.

News of the hospital's work spread quickly. Every night, women appeared at the gates, sometimes by the hundreds. They came as if angels had appeared to them and had declared that, despite the shame and scorn of the world, they should have peace, and the good will of heaven.

There were shepherds abiding in the field,
Keeping watch over their flock by night.
And lo; the angel of the Lord came upon them,
And the glory of the Lord shone round about them,
And they were sore afraid.
And the angel said unto them,
Fear not; for behold, I bring you good tidings of great joy,
Which shall be to all people.
For unto you is born this day, in the City of David,
A Saviour, which is Christ the Lord.
And suddenly there was with the angel
A multitude of the heav'nly host, praising God and saying:
Glory to God in the highest,
And peace on earth.
Good will towards men.

After 1750, *Messiah* continued to be performed each year at the hospital, a tradition that continued for more than twenty years. Thousands of children were gathered, and thousands of women stepped back from a dark precipice. The words of *Messiah* were literally fulfilled—the Good Shepherd had gently led those who were with young.

> *He shall feed his flock like a shepherd:*
> *He shall gather the lambs with his arm,*
> *And carry them in his bosom,*
> *And gently lead those that are with young.*

Jesus said, "By their fruits ye shall know them." The fruits of Handel's *Messiah* were real and abundant—freed debtors, liberated mothers, rescued children. Handel hadn't just told the story of the Messiah—the Redeemer. He had actually helped to do the Messiah's work: to succor God's children and save them from spiritual death. For each of these precious souls, the Redeemer lived.

> *I know that my Redeemer liveth . . .*
> *For now is Christ risen from the dead,*
> *The first fruits of them that sleep.*

Handel's work had not only been a blessing to the needy. It had been a call, even a warning to the unsavory, unscrupulous, and unrighteous—a reminder that though weeping may endure for a night, because of the Messiah, joy will come in the morning.

> *He that dwelleth in heaven shall laugh them to scorn.*
> *The Lord shall have them in derision.*
> *Thou shalt break them with a rod of iron;*
> *Thou shalt dash them in pieces like a Potter's vessel.*

When George Frideric Handel set down his pen in mid-September 1741, he could not have imagined how influential *Messiah* would become.

Eighteen years later, a few days after hearing a performance of *Messiah*, Handel died. But his music did not. Today, his body of work is performed around the world, yet none of it more frequently or more universally than *Messiah*.

There are many reasons for its success, but perhaps, as the Bible explains, "the greatest of these is charity"—to feed the hungry, clothe the naked, liberate the captive, administer relief to the sick and the afflicted, and minister to every needy soul.

This, then, is the "spirit of Christmas." It is ours whenever we heed the wondrous invitation of *Messiah* to be charitable to others. And when we do, we are changed. We are filled with Christmas peace and hope and joy. Which is why we sing—at Christmastime and throughout the year—"Hallelujah!"

May it ever be so.

> *Behold, I tell you a mystery:*
> *We shall not all sleep,*
> *But we shall all be chang'd*
> *In a moment, in the twinkling of an eye,*
> *At the last trumpet.*
>
> *Hallelujah!*
> *For the Lord God Omnipotent reigneth.*
> *The kingdom of this world is become the kingdom of our Lord and of his Christ;*
> *And he shall reign for ever and ever,*
> *King of Kings,*
> *And Lord of Lords.*
> *Hallelujah!*

THE LITTLE MATCH GIRL

A Retelling of the Hans Christian Andersen Story

NARRATED BY ROLANDO VILLAZÓN

On this holy night
All heaven sweetly smiled
When angels gathered 'round
To welcome heaven's child.
May we this Christmas eve,
As angels at His birth,
Enfold each precious child
In love and peace on earth.

It was nearly nightfall. The orphan girl blinked away thick snowflakes falling in her eyes. Everyone in the great city was bundled and busy, heads down, eyes fixed on the black cobblestones peeking up through packed snow. A wagon spewed freezing slush across the girl's loosely wrapped feet.

"Out of the way," its heavy wheels grumbled. But the shivering child was not afraid and did not step back. She stood bravely, silently, holding out all she had in the world— her last bundle of wooden matches, saved for selling this Christmas Eve.

As the tide of darkness rose in side streets and alleyways, the throngs ebbed across courtyards, around corners, and down dimly lit passageways.

Pushed along by the frosty wind, they hurried home for their Christmas giving, passing the little match girl, unaware.

When finally only stray dogs crisscrossed the empty streets, the frail girl retreated to

a corner between two stone houses. Sliding down against the cold wall, she tucked her matches in her pocket and her hands under her arms, lifted her knees, and warmed her face in the shreds of a threadbare apron. But she couldn't look down for long. The Christmas stars above were calling her to look up and out. As she did, she spied the yellow light of a gas lamp, burning atop its cast-iron post. It was a small but steady flame, like the faith that flickered in her heart. If only she could climb up and warm herself in its glow.

But wait, she thought, digging into her apron pocket. *I already have a fire of my own!* Drawing a single match from the bundle, she rubbed the tip along the stone wall. *Whischt!* In an instant, the match was blazing before her. As she held her hand in front of the flame, she found herself basking in the glow of a radiant stove. Nearby, a kindly woman was filling the kindling basket, to keep the fire burning. And for the first time, the little match girl felt she was not alone.

The child stretched out her feet. "Ahhh. At last," she said with a smile. Firelight kissed her delicate fingers and toes, and she wiggled them with delight. The air itself enfolded her in a soft blanket of kindness.

In the Christmas chill,
A spark becomes a flame
When Christmas gifts of love
Bespeak the season's name.
For Christmas is a fire
That melts the fearful soul,
And warms the wounded heart,
And makes the spirit whole.

But as her eyes closed in relief, the match blew out and the fire disappeared. "No! No! Come back!" she cried. Plunging her hands into her apron, she seized another match. *Just one more*, she thought, hoping to make the friendly hearth reappear.

Whischt! Again, a long golden flame reached up before the child. As she studied its graceful curl, bright lights flickered in her shining eyes. She imagined she was staring into the glow of a magnificent chandelier. Suddenly, the wall of the stone house became transparent, like a veil, and she could see a stately dining room within. Fir garlands, parchment decorations, and Christmas candles adorned the elegant hall. The same gentle woman was laying the table—a soft white cloth, a porcelain platter, a roast goose, and sweet bread brimming with spices and candied fruit. For a moment, the child's lips parted with wonder.

When the cupboard's bare
And we've no Christmas feast,
Humility is born,
And gratitude increased.
Then let our bounty be
A fount of grace and love
For all whom God would feed
With mercy from above.

But again, as the little girl closed her eyes to breathe in the savory aroma, a snow-flake landed on the match, and a wisp of smoke rose into the night air and vanished. "Come back, come back," she whispered.

Frantically, she reached for another match. Before she could stop herself, she was striking it against the wall. *Whischt!* In the flash of light, she saw a sparkling silver orna-ment. It was held by a woman's graceful hands and carefully placed on the green boughs of a towering Christmas tree. Slowly the child lifted her eyes—up, up, up. A thousand candle lights. A hundred thousand facets of beauty and wonder and joy. Stars dancing in the sky. *Yes*, she thought, *this is heaven.*

> *When the leaves have flown*
> *And every branch is bare,*
> *A Christmas tree is life*
> *For all souls everywhere.*
> *So lift your eyes and see*
> *This tree of life and light,*
> *That shines as heaven's star,*
> *Upon that holy night.*

Even as the child gasped with delight, her eyes closed and the match went out. The brilliant stars tumbled down, and in their shimmering tails the great tree disappeared.

Bowing her head, she pushed her frozen chin into her chest, where warm tears pooled. Some drops fell onto her freezing hands, and instinctively she covered the last of her matches. A fire in the stove, a feast on the table, candles on the tree. *How could these be gone?* she wondered. There was something real in them. Something alive. Something waiting.

Believing as only a child can, she lifted the remaining bundle of matches and spoke to them simply: "Can you bring Christmas back? Can you give me that beautiful world again?" With a prayer pounding in her heart, she boldly scraped the cluster of tips against the wall—all of them at once. *Whischt!* For a moment, nothing came. But then, slowly, a single flame took hold and burst into a bouquet of fire.

As the little match girl peered into the blaze, she heard a voice she remembered from long ago. "Come, little one." She knew this rustling of skirts, this soft, sweet fragrance.

"Grandmother," she whispered, turning around. "You're here!"

With a tender sigh, the woman sank to her knees. "As I have always been."

Then, like a great swan spreading her wings, the woman wrapped her granddaughter in a shawl of pure white wool. The shreds of the child's gray dress miraculously became a white, gossamer gown. Grandmother took her tiny hand, now beautifully pink and perfectly clean, and drew her close.

"I have come to you, my child, so you can come with me."

As they rose silently into the night, the child felt warmth flow into her feet

and legs. Her dress was full now, with petticoats flowing and a pretty blue sash dancing in the winter wind. She looked out. The new white snow sparkled across rooftops as far as she could see, and moonlight transformed the river into a silvery satin ribbon.

For just a moment the little match girl looked down into the corner between the two stone houses. Alas, a waif was resting quietly against the wall, burned-out matchsticks scattered around her, a smile of perfect contentment on her lips.

When I come back, I will bring that brave child more Christmas matches, she thought to herself. *I'll bring a whole bundle of them!*

Squeezing her grandmother's hand, she looked up into the warm, lustrous light. Stars were gathering in the open portals, waiting to dance with her for joy. She would never look down again.

The next morning, people passing by glanced at the child's body and turned their eyes away. They could only imagine she had been abandoned there, alone in the darkness. But the truth is, she was never alone. She had drawn on the light she had—on everything within her—to kindle the visions of Christmas. And in return, Christmas had brought her the love of family, the mercy of heaven, and a pathway home. As thick snowflakes fell in the little match girl's eyes, her tears were washed away. And the fire in her heart burned on, bright and strong, forever.

> *On this holy night*
> *Once host to heaven's joy,*
> *The angels gathered 'round*
> *To welcome heaven's boy.*
> *May we this Christmas eve,*
> *As angels at His birth,*
> *Proclaim His holy love*
> *And sing His peace on earth!*

IT IS WELL WITH MY SOUL

The Spirit of Christmas through One Family's

Unforgettable Journey

NARRATED BY HUGH BONNEVILLE

This is a true story about a family at Christmastime—a mother and father who, in the night of their deepest despair, discovered the healing light of hope.

As it was in Bethlehem, when darkness gathers, the Savior's light shines.

And when His light is reflected in sacred verse and song, the peace of Christmas, the real Spirit of the Season, lifts and comforts and blesses us all.

In mid-November 1873, an ocean liner, the *Ville du Havre*, set sail from New York with 313 passengers on board. One can imagine their festive Atlantic crossing with ribbons of red, swags of evergreen, and Christmas carols wafting through a dining room sparkling with candlelight. In a few days they would make landfall in Europe, just weeks before Christmas in Paris.

Anna Spafford and her four little girls were among the happy passengers. They had come from Chicago—Annie, age eleven; Margaret Lee, nine; Bessie, five; and little Tanetta, two. Their father, Horatio, had intended to sail with them but was detained on business. "Not to worry," he assured his wife and children. He would book his passage in a few days, and soon they would be reunited in the City of Light, celebrating the season of joy. And joy is what they needed. Two years earlier, the Great Chicago Fire had all but destroyed Horatio's business interests. This journey was intended to restore hope and bring healing into the Spaffords' lives—which is why on the ship, on the evening of

November twenty-second, Anna and her girls knelt down, said prayers for peace, and fell asleep, dreaming of the yuletide festivities to come.

At about two o'clock in the morning, they were jolted awake in their berths. Despite the night's clear, starry sky, the *Ville du Havre* had inexplicably collided with the *Loch Earn*, an iron-hulled Scottish clipper. Lifeboats quickly filled with people. Many passengers leapt into the icy waters. Anna tried desperately to keep her children together, but the two eldest became separated in the confusion. Just twelve minutes after the impact, a wave washed over the deck and Anna was drawn under the water with her youngest daughters.

She held on to five-year-old Bessie until her strength gave out. Her last memory was of two-year-old Tanetta, in her delicate lace nightgown, torn from her grasp, getting smaller and smaller until she, too, finally disappeared. Later, the crew of the *Loch Earn* found Anna unconscious, floating on a wooden plank.

When the ship docked in Wales, Anna sent a telegram to her husband that began with the words, "Saved alone, what shall I do?"

Horatio immediately sailed from New York City. "There is just one thing in these days that has become magnificently clear," he wrote to a friend. "I must not lose faith."

Four days into his voyage, on a Thursday evening, the captain summoned Mr. Spafford to the foredeck. By the crew's calculations, they were nearing the place where Anna's ship had gone down, taking with it the bodies of their four daughters, now resting some three miles below. But Horatio refused to look down.

"I did not think of our dear ones there," he later recounted. Instead, he gazed out across the rolling waves and up into the moonlit sky. There he began to formulate a simple expression of his faith—a verse that would become a beloved hymn.

> *When peace like a river attendeth my way,*
> *When sorrows like sea billows roll,*
> *Whatever my lot, Thou hast taught me to say,*
> *It is well, it is well with my soul.*

Only a few weeks earlier, in the same place on the open sea, Anna had experienced a similar awakening. After her rescue, when she regained consciousness, she was overcome with despair and wanted to throw herself back into the ocean. What was life worth now, and what could it ever be without her beloved children? But then, it was as if she heard a voice in her mind and her heart: "You are spared for a purpose, Anna. You have a work to do."

The couple returned to Chicago, where Horatio sought the support and prayers of his congregation to help him face the dire financial straits in which he found himself. Anna gave birth to a boy and then a girl. But—sorrow upon sorrow—that son, Horatio Jr., succumbed to scarlet fever at the age of three. Then, a year later, another daughter was born. Although only two of their seven children lived to maturity, the Spaffords never yielded hope.

Through that harrowing Christmas season of 1873, and in the years that followed, Horatio and Anna became even more certain that God loves *all* His children, whoever they are and whatever tribulations they may suffer.

In 1881, they moved their family to Jerusalem and established what they called the American Colony, not far from the "Little Town of Bethlehem" we celebrate at Christmas. Although they were deeply religious, their purpose was not to proselytize but to serve people of all backgrounds, relieving the effects of poverty, disease, and strife wherever they were found.

Seven years later, Horatio died. Once again, Anna Spafford had reason to give up, but she did not. Every life has contradictions and imperfections, and hers was no exception. Yet, when it mattered most, in her most profound spiritual crisis, when all seemed lost, Anna found the strength to move forward and to turn outward—to continue what she and her husband had begun. And the seed of service they planted in others bore sweet fruit, indeed.

In time, their daughter Bertha greatly expanded the Spaffords' humanitarian work, all with the intent of rescuing those who had experienced the shipwrecks of life. During World War I, she led the way in organizing soup kitchens for refugees. She also oversaw hospitals for wounded soldiers on all sides of the conflict.

One Christmas Eve, on her way to Bethlehem, Bertha met a Bedouin man, his ailing wife, and their newborn son traveling to Jerusalem by donkey. Later she wrote, "Here stood before me a rustic Madonna and babe, and similar to Mary's plight, there was no place for them to stay." By the next morning the mother had died, and Bertha was asked to care for the child. She agreed. She named the little boy Noel. Within the week she had taken in two more orphaned babies. And so began the Spafford family's most enduring charitable work—a renowned hospital for children.

Bertha explained, "We make no distinction in nationality or creed. The only

requirement being that people absolutely need our help." Some of the Spaffords' charitable work continues to this day—in the children's center that bears their family name.

For nearly 150 years, millions have sung and have been lifted by Horatio's hymn, "It
Is Well with My Soul." Most have been unaware of the circumstances in which it was
written, but they have been strengthened by its universal message. Horatio's words resound with the truth we celebrate at Christmas: a child was born in Bethlehem, bringing
peace on earth and good will toward men. Because of Him, the human spirit can rise
above tragedy. Whenever, however we suffer our own night of sorrow, His love does
shine in the darkness. His peace can heal the wounded soul. And the Christmas work of
giving, loving, serving, and rescuing is ours, if we choose to make it so. As we do, we join
with saints and angels to rejoice and sing: "It is well, it is well with my soul!"

IT IS WELL WITH MY SOUL

By Horatio Gates Spafford

When peace like a river attendeth my way,
When sorrows like sea billows roll,
Whatever my lot, Thou hast taught me to say,
It is well, it is well with my soul.

Though Satan should buffet, though trials should come,
Let this blest assurance control,
That Christ hath regarded my helpless estate,
And hath shed His own blood for my soul.

My sin—oh, the bliss of this glorious thought!—
My sin, not in part but the whole,
Is nailed to the cross, and I bear it no more,
Praise the Lord, praise the Lord, O my soul!

For me, be it Christ, be it Christ hence to live:
If Jordan above me shall roll,
No pang shall be mine, for in death as in life,
Thou wilt whisper Thy peace to my soul.

But, Lord, 'tis for Thee, for Thy coming we wait;
The sky, not the grave, is our goal;
Oh, trump of the angel! Oh, voice of the Lord!
Blessed hope, blessed rest of my soul!

And, Lord, haste the day when the faith shall be sight,
The clouds be rolled back as a scroll;
The trump shall resound, and the Lord shall descend,
Even so, it is well with my soul.

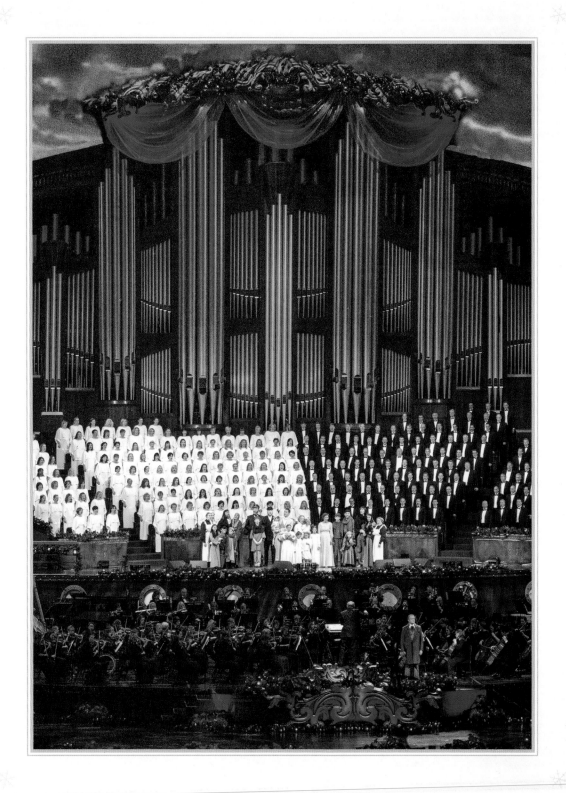

THE GIFT OF THE MAGI

A New Rendition of the O. Henry Classic

NARRATED BY KRISTIN CHENOWETH

M r. and Mrs. James and Della Young were so poor, they could barely afford their furnished flat at eight dollars a week, so there was no possibility of them giving gifts to each other that Christmas.

Della had secretly saved one dollar and eighty-seven cents. But it was not nearly enough to buy James a chain for his prized pocket watch.

And James had no money to buy Della what she had been yearning for—a pair of pure tortoiseshell combs with jeweled rims, just the right shade for holding back her long, wavy, chestnut-brown hair.

But Della and Jim could not bear to celebrate Christmas without giving each other at least one gift. So, taking no thought for themselves, each found a way.

Which is why, the day before Christmas, when Jim walked through the door, he stopped—immoveable as an Irish setter at the scent of quail. Della's hair was gone. Vanished. And all that was left were the tiny, close-lying curls of a truant schoolboy, or a Coney Island chorus girl.

"Jim, darling," she cried, "don't look at me that way. I had my hair cut off and sold because I couldn't have lived through Christmas without giving you a present."

"You cut off your hair?" he said, with an air of near lunacy.

"It's sold! Sold and gone, I tell you. Say, 'Merry Christmas!' Jim, and let's be happy.

Maybe the hairs of my head were numbered, but nobody . . . nobody could ever count my love for you."

At that, Jim quickly woke from his trance and enfolded Della in his arms.

Now, here Mr. O. Henry pauses to ask a question: Eight dollars a week or a million dollars a year—what's the difference? Even an accountant would give you the wrong answer. For what made the gifts of the Magi valuable was not the cost of their treasures, but the distance they traveled and the risk they took.

Now, back to the story. Relaxing his embrace, Jim drew a package from his overcoat pocket and threw it on the table. "Don't make any mistake about me, Dell," he said. "I don't think there's anything in the way of a haircut or a shave or a shampoo that could make me love my girl any less. But if you'll unwrap that package . . ."

Della's white, nimble fingers tore at the string and paper. There was an ecstatic scream of joy; and then, alas, a quick change to tears and wails. For there lay "The Combs"—the set of combs, side and back, that Della had so long worshipped in a shop window. And now they were hers, but the cascading tresses they were meant to adorn were gone. Della hugged the combs to her bosom, and at length looked up with dim eyes: "My hair grows so fast, Jim."

Then, leaping like a singed cat, Della scooped up her gift for Jim and held it out in her open palm. The precious metal seemed to flash with a reflection of her bright and ardent spirit. "Isn't it a dandy chain, Jim? I hunted all over town to find it. You'll have to look at your watch a hundred times a day now."

Jim just tumbled down on the couch, put his hands under the back of his head, and smiled. "Dell," he said, "let's put our Christmas presents away and keep 'em a while. They're just too nice to use right now. I sold my watch to buy your combs. And now, I think, it's time for dinner."

The best gifts do not come in packages. What makes them valuable is not what they cost to buy, but what they cost to give. The Child in Bethlehem gave a gift not even kings could afford: His perfect life and pure love for all.

As Mr. O. Henry observed, "The Magi were wise men—wonderfully wise men—who brought gifts to the Babe in the manger." And tonight, we have recounted the story of two brave and innocent children who foolishly sacrificed their treasures for one another! But they were not foolish. They were wise. And the faithful spouse, the hopeful parent, the loving family, the trusted friend—they are all wise in the same way. For they give of themselves. They give Christmas. They *are* the Magi.

CHRISTMAS DAY IN THE MORNING

An Adaptation of Pearl S. Buck's Beloved Narrative

NARRATED BY RICHARD THOMAS

Robert woke suddenly and completely. It was four o'clock, the hour when his father had always called him to get up and help with the milking. That was fifty years ago, but his eyes still opened every morning at four. And even if he wanted to go back to sleep—which he usually did—it wasn't going to happen this morning, because this morning was Christmas.

He looked at his wife sleeping beside him and remembered Christmases when their children were young. This had been a joyous day—the day she labored and lived for, filled with the laughter of little ones. But now those children were grown and the house was empty, and for her Christmas was becoming just another winter morning, its joy a memory of the past. His mind slipped back further, to growing up on his father's farm. He had always loved his father, but he hadn't realized how much. And then one day he overheard his parents talking.

"I wish I didn't have to get Robby up so early," his father said. "He's growin' so fast, and he needs his sleep. If I could just find a way to handle the milkin' alone . . ."

"Well, you can't," his mother said firmly. "Besides, he's not a child anymore, and it's time he do his part."

"It's true," said his father. "But I still don't like to wake him."

Hearing those words, something awakened in Rob. His father loved him! He had never thought of it before, but now he knew it. And he could never go back to waiting

for his father to call him in the mornings, again and again. He might stumble out of bed blind with sleep, pulling on his clothes with his eyes half shut. But he would get up.

A few days later, on Christmas Eve, Rob was lying in his bed thinking about the next morning. His family was poor, and most of their excitement was about the turkey they raised themselves and mince pies his mother made.

His parents always gave him something he needed, and he saved to buy them gifts, too. For his father, it was always a tie from the ten-cent store. But that Christmas, the tie just wasn't enough. Rob had to give him something better—something more.

Rob lay on his side, propped up on one elbow, looking out the attic window. The stars were bright, much brighter than he ever remembered them. And he wondered if one of them was the star that shone over Bethlehem.

O watch the stars, see how they run.
O watch the stars, see how they run.
The stars run down at the setting of the sun.
O watch the stars, see how they run.

"Dad," Rob once asked when he was a little boy, "what's a stable?"

"It's just a barn," his father had replied, "like ours."

So, Jesus had been born in a barn! And to a barn the shepherds had come, and Wise Men with their gifts. In that moment, a thought struck Rob like lightning: They had a barn, and in it there was a gift for him to give. He would get up before four o'clock and milk the cows. He'd do it alone, while everyone was asleep, and when his father opened the barn door, all the work would be done. A smile broke across Rob's face and his eyes danced with the stars.

Go find the Child, see where He lies.
Go find the Child, see where He lies.
He sweetly lies wrapped in Mary's lullabies.
Go find the Child, see where He lies.

Rob must have woken twenty times that night, scratching a match each time to look at his old watch. Midnight. One o'clock. Half past two. At a quarter to three he finally got up and put on his clothes, crept downstairs (being careful of the creaky boards), and let himself out.

Inside the barn, he lit the old hurricane lamp. The cows were looking at him, sleepy and surprised. It was early for them, too. Then, with a great rush of energy, Rob set to work. He smiled as he milked steadily, two strong streams rushing into the pail, frothing and fragrant. For once, milking was not a chore. It was something else—a gift to his father who loved him.

When he finished, the two milk cans were perfectly full. He covered them and closed the milk house door carefully, making sure of the latch.

Back in his room he had only a minute to pull off his clothes in the darkness and jump into bed. His father was already coming down the hall. Rob yanked the covers over his head as the door opened.

"Rob! We have to get up, son . . ."

"Aw-right," he mumbled.

The door closed and Rob lay still, breathing heavily. In just a few minutes his father would know. His heart was ready to jump from his body.

The minutes seemed endless—ten, fifteen, he didn't know how many—until he heard his father's footsteps. Again, the door opened.

"Robert!"

"Yes, Dad—"

His father was laughing, a strange sobbing sort of laugh. "Thought you'd fool me, did you?" His father was standing by his bed, feeling for him, pulling away the covers.

"It's for Christmas!" Rob cried, finding his father and clutching him in a great hug. He felt his father's arms around him in the dark.

"Son, I thank you. Nobody ever did a nicer thing—"

"Oh, Dad," Rob said, "I just want to be good!" The words broke from him of their own will. His heart was bursting with joy.

Fifty years later, Robert reflected on that Christmas, and again something in him awakened. He looked over at his wife and remembered the years of Christmas mornings she had made joyous for him and their children. In that moment, all he wanted was to give her something, to do something to express his love and revive their joy.

And then it struck him like lightning: The true joy of Christmas is to love and to awaken love. Their children were grown and their house was empty, and the laughter of

little ones would remain a memory. And yet, because of his father's love, and because of hers, love was alive in him. And the joy of Christmas was his to give.

Quietly, he got up in the dark, pulled on his clothes as he had done so many years before, and crept to his desk (being careful of the creaky boards). "My dearest love," he wrote, his pen flowing freely across milk-white paper.

On this Christmas day, on this Christmas day in the morning . . .

Merry Christmas, my love.

Your husband, Rob.

Behold the Lamb, see how He loves.
Behold the Lamb, see how He loves.
The Lamb loves you, and will bring you home above.

O watch the stars,
Go find the Child,
Behold the Lamb, see how He loves!

CHRISTMAS WITH THE TABERNACLE CHOIR AT TEMPLE SQUARE

Every December, one of the many wonders of Christmas in Salt Lake City is the annual concert of The Tabernacle Choir and Orchestra at Temple Square, a Temple Square tradition for decades. Since 2000, these popular concerts have delighted live audiences of over 60,000 people each year in the Conference Center of The Church of Jesus Christ of Latter-day Saints, with millions more tuning in to *Christmas with The Tabernacle Choir* on PBS through the partnership of GBH and BYU Television. It is a full-scale production featuring world-class musicians, soloists, dancers, narrators, and music that delights viewers each year.

Each concert has featured a special guest artist, including Broadway actors and singers Kelli O'Hara (2019), Kristin Chenoweth (2018), Sutton Foster (2017), Laura Osnes (2015), Santino Fontana (2014), Alfie Boe (2012), and Brian Stokes Mitchell (2008); opera stars Rolando Villazón (2016), Deborah Voigt (2013), Nathan Gunn (2011), Renée Fleming (2005), Bryn Terfel (2003), and Frederica von Stade (2003); Grammy Award–winner Natalie Cole (2009), *American Idol* finalist David Archuleta (2010); and the Muppets® from Sesame Street® (2014). The remarkable talents of award-winning actors Richard Thomas (2019), Hugh Bonneville (2017), Martin Jarvis (2015), John Rhys-Davies (2013), Jane Seymour (2011), Michael York (2010), and Edward Herrmann (2008) have graced the stage, sharing memorable stories of the season. Featured narrators also include famed broadcast journalist Tom Brokaw (2012), two-time Pulitzer Prize–winning author David McCullough (2009), and noted TV news anchorman Walter Cronkite (2002).

The 360 members of The Tabernacle Choir represent men and women from many different backgrounds and professions and range in age from twenty-five to sixty. Their companion ensemble, the Orchestra at Temple Square, includes a roster of more than 200 musicians who accompany the Choir on broadcasts, recordings, and tours. All serve as unpaid volunteers with a mission of sharing inspired music that has the power to bring people closer to the divine. The Bells at Temple Square, a 32-member handbell choir established in 2005, adds a particular sparkle to the concerts each year.

The Tabernacle Choir has appeared at thirteen world's fairs and expositions, performed at the inaugurations of seven U.S. presidents, and sung for numerous worldwide telecasts and special events. Five of The Tabernacle Choir's recordings have achieved "gold record" and two have achieved "platinum record" status. Its recordings have reached the #1 position on Billboard® magazine's classical lists a remarkable thirteen times since 2003. Today, music from the Choir and Orchestra is available on demand, across the world, through the Choir's own digital channels and other major streaming services.

For more information about these Christmas concerts and available performance videos, please visit TabChoir.org/KeepsakeChristmas.

ACKNOWLEDGMENTS AND COPYRIGHT INFORMATION

All of these stories were written or adapted for The Tabernacle Choir at Temple Square for Christmas concerts held in the Conference Center of The Church of Jesus Christ of Latter-day Saints in Salt Lake City, Utah. The Tabernacle Choir gratefully acknowledges the creative contributions of thousands of volunteers and production professionals who helped make these stories an inspiring part of its annual Christmas concerts over the past twenty years.

Silent Night, Holy Night: The Story of the World War I Christmas Truce
Written by David T. Warner based on work by Stephen Wunderli
© 2003 Intellectual Reserve, Inc. All rights reserved.

A Christmas Bell for Anya: An Original Russian Christmas Tale
Written by Chris and Evie Stewart
© 2006 Chris Stewart and Evie Stewart

Longfellow's Christmas: The Inspiring Origins of "I Heard the Bells on Christmas Day"
Written by David T. Warner based on work by Lloyd and Karmel Newell
© 2009 Intellectual Reserve, Inc. All rights reserved.

In the Dark Streets Shineth: A 1941 Christmas Eve Story
Written by David McCullough
© 2010 Intellectual Reserve, Inc. All rights reserved.

Sing, Choirs of Angels! The Beginnings of The Tabernacle Choir
Written by David T. Warner
Performance © 2010 Intellectual Reserve, Inc. All rights reserved.
Text © 2021 Intellectual Reserve, Inc. All rights reserved.

Good King Wenceslas: The Hidden Parable in the Familiar Carol
Written by David T. Warner
© 2012 Intellectual Reserve, Inc. All rights reserved.

Christmas from Heaven: The True Story of the Berlin Candy Bomber
Written by David T. Warner
© 2013 Intellectual Reserve, Inc. All rights reserved.

God Bless Us, Every One! Imagining How Dickens's Carol *Came to Be*
Written by David T. Warner
© 2014 Intellectual Reserve, Inc. All rights reserved.

For unto Us: The Wondrous Invitation of Handel's Messiah
Written by David T. Warner
Performance © 2015 Intellectual Reserve, Inc. All rights reserved.
Text © 2021 Intellectual Reserve, Inc. All rights reserved.

The Little Match Girl: A Retelling of the Hans Christian Andersen Story
Written by Hans Christian Andersen; adapted by David T. Warner
Adaptation © 2017 Intellectual Reserve, Inc. All rights reserved.

It Is Well with My Soul: The Spirit of Christmas through One Family's Unforgettable Journey
Written by David T. Warner
© 2018 Intellectual Reserve, Inc. All rights reserved.

The Gift of the Magi: A New Rendition of the O. Henry Classic
Written by O. Henry; adapted by David T. Warner
Performance © 2018 Intellectual Adaptation © 2021 Intellectual Reserve, Inc. All rights reserved.

Christmas Day in the Morning: An Adaptation of Pearl S. Buck's Beloved Narrative
Written by Pearl S. Buck; adapted by David T. Warner
Adaptation © 2020 Intellectual Reserve, Inc. All rights reserved.

For contributions to this book, the Choir expresses its thanks and appreciation for photography provided by the *Deseret News* and by Choir photographers Ron Crapo, Deb Gehris, and Ed Thompson; editing by Lisa Mangum; legal coordination by Carol Newton for the Choir and Jack Newman for Shadow Mountain; guest artist coordination by Ron Gunnell, Executive Vice President-Talent for the Choir; product direction by Chris Schoebinger at Shadow Mountain; and executive direction by Scott Barrick, Choir General Manager.